PHOTOGRAPHERS' BRITAIN

OXFORDSHIRE

To
Audrey McBeath,
my mother,
who died too soon.

PHOTOGRAPHERS' BRITAIN

OXFORDSHIRE

NORMAN McBEATH

ALAN SUTTON

OXFORDSHIRE BOOKS

First Published in the United Kingdom in 1992
Alan Sutton Publishing Ltd · Phoenix Mill · Far Thrupp · Stroud · Gloucestershire

Oxfordshire Books · Oxfordshire County Council
Leisure and Arts · Central Library · Westgate · Oxford

First published in the United States of America in 1992
Alan Sutton Publishing Inc · Wolfeboro Falls · NH 03896–0848

British Library Cataloguing in Publication Data

McBeath, Norman
Photographers' Britain: Oxfordshire
I. Title
779.94257

ISBN 0-7509-0072-5

Library of Congress Cataloging in Publication Data applied for

Cover photograph: Rollright Stones

Endpapers: Spires of Oxford

Title page photograph: Godstow Nunnery

Typeset in 10/14 Sabon.
Typesetting and origination by
Alan Sutton Publishing Limited.
Printed in Great Britain by
The Bath Press, Bath, Avon.

ACKNOWLEDGEMENTS

Producing a book of this nature involves two quite solitary activities, writing and photography. At the end of the day nobody else can hold the pen and the camera's viewfinder is designed for use by one eye. However, this is nowhere near the whole story. Well before either activity can start, the task is dispersed over a great many individuals. It is their help and contributions that enable the work to take off in the first place and that frequently take care of the inevitable areas of turbulence along the way.

It is one thing to consult a reference book but there can be no substitute for first hand knowledge of an area. For alerting me to all kinds of treasures I am most indebted to Michael Black, Helen Howgego and Anthony Stones.

After gathering information about a site comes the visit. This invariably involves asking help from yet more people even if it is just to go through a gate, get directions or have a chat about the place. All such assistance was of great importance to me and very much appreciated. I always expected people to be hostile to a wandering snapper so it was doubly pleasing to have been met in all instances with courtesy and kindness. For such help I am most grateful.

To transform my perceptions into tangible form I am indebted to Keith Barnes of The Photographers Workshop in Oxford for processing facilities and much time under red light. Paddy Summerfield, with his ever keen eye and wealth of experience deserves much thanks for influence and help with seeing and printing. At this stage must also be mentioned Jaqueline Mitchell, my editor. In no small measure do her skills and patience bear directly on the successful completion of this book. Then there are those who have been privy to the inevitable anxieties that come with such a project. All have given me encouragement throughout for which I will always be grateful. I would specially like to mention Helen Wedgwood who was asked more of than most.

Finally, I must record special thanks to Jenny Cooper for her unfailing encouragement and seemingly boundless energy and talent for research. Her considerable efforts helped me from the first day till the last.

LEAFIELD

INTRODUCTION

Some hold the view that the true nature of things is best revealed through an examination of detail, of constituent parts and of sections. From this, so the argument runs, a synthesis of elements can take place and give a more authentic and valid notion of the whole. This collection of photographs is, to some extent, a reflection of that view. Although each image should stand on its own, I hope as a group they provide an insight into the character of this particular area of the United Kingdom.

The only qualification to this is that they are very much my own view and so the content is an idiosyncratic one. However, I make no apologies for this. This is not a guidebook nor does it attempt to provide a thorough and exhaustive coverage of the county. For this reason there will be places of great interest that have neither been mentioned nor photographed. Conversely, I have given space to little corners that made a great impression on me but which few people except locals will know of. Besides, there are already plenty of images of the most noteworthy places and the potential of this book would have been greatly undermined by simply looking for new angles on familiar subjects. Where this has been done, particularly in photographs within Oxford itself, the incentive for inclusion developed from the plethora of hackneyed images that are so much in evidence.

With one exception there are no people in any of the photographs. For me this is strange in that I have always found people fascinating and spend a lot of time photographing them in a number of contexts. However, for such a topic I felt that they would only serve as a distraction . More than that, I wanted to provide something of a balance in being able to concentrate not so much on the oft talked about 'moment' but on the form and light within each frame. I think this comes better across in that other moment, the instance *before* people arrive or just *after* they have left.

Whether people or not, I would hope that these photographs might draw attention to features of the environment that are all too often missed and which might be more appreciated. I had the valuable opportunity to spend the time and, at the end of the day, can only hope that they are worth somebody's time to look at.

Norman McBeath
May, 1992, Oxford

BLISS'S MILL AT CHIPPING NORTON

Chipping Norton is in the north-west corner of the county and is very much a Cotswold market town. Its name, derived from an Old English word for market, betrays much of its history, but not all.

From name to fame is what this picture might be called, with textiles the work that gained the reputation. This is of some consequence as agriculture and the manufacture of cloth are the oldest industries in Oxfordshire. The shift in emphasis came in 1746 when Bliss's mill was set up to make webs and horsecloth for the coach traffic which passed through the town on its way between Worcester and Oxford: a busy route even then. About a hundred years later the company changed production to making serges and tweeds for which it received international acclaim. The mill pictured opposite illustrates the Victorian Versailles style and was opened in 1872 at a cost of £80,000. High quality tweed production continued until 1980. It is now being converted into flats.

This building is an obvious landmark from the A44 to Evesham as it leaves the town. It sits perfectly in a small valley, very much a part of the geography. This is how I remember the first time I came across the mill and in photographing it I wanted to emphasize the definitive feature, that powerful central chimney.

ASHMOLEAN MUSEUM

Oxford, in many ways, is a city of cosy proportions that strangely belies its immense stature and worldwide reputation. Little doors lead to little porters' lodges which guard the way to little corridors and quads. Everything is of a manageable size and provides a pleasing reminder of the argument against today's pre-occupation with expansion and growth.

This museum with its uncluttered and lofty neo-classical façade is a quiet departure from the proportions of most of the university buildings. No turrets, gargoyles or arched doorways can be seen here. Partly as a consequence, you have an ideal receptor for the light that can illuminate flat, creamy-white surfaces that make the building glow. This is particularly evident in the morning when the central portico shines as if in sympathy with the treasures that lie behind.

Housed in this, the oldest public museum in Britain, are paintings by Rubens, Rembrandt, Pissarro, Van Gogh and Picasso to name just the obvious. Other exhibits include Egyptian mummies, Anglo-Saxon jewellery, Greek statues and even Guy Fawkes's lantern.

Although there is often a banner unfurled which proclaims its foundation in 1683, the need for signs and notices to tempt me in is very much eclipsed by the luminescent grandure that I look forward to seeing when the sun is shining in Beaumont Street.

GREAT TEW

Great Tew is one of three Tews, all quite close to one another but each with its own character. This particular village has featured in a number of films and television series, location scouts having been attracted by the definitively picturesque rows of thatched cottages. It immediately made me think of jigsaws and chocolate boxes and was a bit of a shock as I had somehow never really imagined that such places exist. It was so well laid out that it was not surprising to learn that it had been carefully landscaped. The designer was J.C. Loudon and his work was carried out in the early part of the nineteenth century.

The village pub, 'spoiled neither by man nor time', is named after Viscount Falkland who lived in the large manor house overlooking the village. He was one of the many who died fighting for King Charles I at the battle of Newbury in 1643. When he fell he was only thirty-three.

Above and to the south of the village is the ancient church of St Michael and All Angels. The church has a rich history and a host of interesting features. For instance, towards the east and along the outside wall are a number of Scratch-Dials. In medieval times these were used like sundials to give the time of the next mass.

Within such a rich environment I found it difficult to decide on which aspect to concentrate. Whatever it was going to be I felt it important that the light was good. This narrrowed the choice and it quickly became clear that the cottages, the hallmark of this village, would provide the strongest image.

SIGNPOST

I have always thought that of the many features that separate urban from rural one of the most compelling is the timeless quality of the country. In towns, and even more so in cities, there is continuous movement, people are numerous and man-made objects are omnipresent. There is also the pervasive and persistent noise of some kind of machine or device: be it an engine or just a radio broadcast. With all of these come reminders of our place in time. Each one provides a reference to the state of technology and also our own responses to it. We are left in no doubt that it is roughly the end of the twentieth century.

The contrast is immediately apparent when these reminders are left behind. The noise is that of the wind, rustling leaves or birds singing. Trees and plants are, in broad terms at least, the same as they have always been and, in the absence of people, there is precious little to fix a point in time.

Somewhere in between these two positions lies this little gem of rustic hardware for it is clearly linked to a specific period, now gone. The result is that the illusion is created of wandering about in the past, however ephemeral. It was nice to try and capture that feeling of being in another time but no sooner had I reached for the tripod than the bubble was burst by a sudden arrival in the background. At least there is the record of an endangered artefact.

HOOK NORTON BREWERY

Just over a hundred years ago virtually every city in England and many of the larger villages had their own brewery. Although the basic process was no mystery each of the breweries had their preferred techniques of blending, cooling, fermenting and storing thus leading to the production of an extensive range of ales with distinctive flavours and individual strengths.

At this time Oxfordshire itself supported forty-five separate breweries, all very much family affairs. Today only a handful of such establishments remain and this must be one of the finest.

In spite of the imposing façade the building is not at all obvious from the village, sitting discreetly at the top of a hill at the bottom of which is the only obvious clue to its location: the street sign 'Brewery Lane'.

The shapes on this building are fascinating as they are all evidence of an aspect of its functional construction. The cast iron and local ironstone components give it a solidity that is reassuring to look at. But the strongest feature of all must be that during production the building comes alive, enveloped in steam and thudding away to the beat of the steam engine that has been lifting water from the wells since the start of this century.

NORTH LEIGH

Although this picture was taken in North Leigh it is perhaps worthy of remark that the village shares a number of features with its equally interesting namesake a few miles to the south. Both have a number of contemporary housing developments which are in stark contrast to the older and more traditional interiors of the villages. Such differences must surely be a rich source of material and debate for future social historians. The most interesting features are the churches and, in both cases, they can easily be missed.

Leaving aside impressions of the building, the first thing to be evident is the unusual number of stone sarcophagi that populate the graveyard. They create a strong feeling of antiquity which is manifested in the church itself for here can be seen work from each of nine centuries. These range from an eleventh-century Saxon tower through to contemporary work that houses the organ.

There are some subjects that attract a lot of interest from photographers, and churches are one. It was, therefore, a relief to find the opportunity to offer a variation. I also like the idea that it should be the view seen by many leaving the church rather than the conventional one taken on arrival.

ALFRED THE GREAT AT WANTAGE

Alfred found learning dead
and he restored it
Education neglected
and he revived it
The laws powerless
and he gave them force
The church debased
and he raised it
The land ravaged by a fearful enemy
from which he delivered it.

A little reminiscent of the text sometimes seen on electioneering pamphlets these lines appear below the statue of King Alfred the Great testifying to some of his achievements. Born at Wantage in 849, he was the first real king of the English. His victory over the invading Danish forces along with his reputation for scholarship forged his reputation and is why he stands bold, with axe and scroll.

The statue is in the centre of the market square, the market being another aspect of the town which is prominent in its history. It has been established for seven centuries during which time it developed into an important trading centre for this area of the Vale of White Horse. Such was its development that about a hundred years before this gleaming white statue was erected, rowdy behaviour and much drunkenness led to the town being known as 'black Wantage'.

THE GREAT BARN

The leaflet produced by the National Trust quotes a noted authority as saying that this barn is 'the finest of the surviving medieval barns in England, amd one of the most impressive structures of its kind in the whole of Europe'.

Its size alone is perhaps enough to convince even the most sceptical of laymen as to the validity of such a statement. This thing is over 150 feet long, all but 50 feet high and 44 feet wide. It was also built over seven hundred years ago and so skilfully that of the two rows of oak posts on which the roofing frames rest not one has shifted from its original position. Another testimonial for the opening quote came for me when I saw that the barn was still in use and full of contemporary farm machinery.

I feel that form is an important feature in most photographs and that is very much what I was struck by when I first came across this building. It's very size and apparent simple construction meant that shape was what preoccupied me when I moved to the blinkered view offered through the viewfinder.

RYCOTE CHAPEL

It is one thing to try and steer the gods in your favour by making a wish now and then, or carrying one of the wealth of good luck charms that are available. But imagine employing a team of clerics whose prime responsibility was to pray for your soul. This is precisely what was done by Richard Quartermayne, Lord of the Manor, when in 1449 he had this little chapel built. It is also a chantry, a term that refers to an endowment or building set up for just that purpose.

There are a number of striking features about this gem, the most basic being that it stands as originally built. Another is the interior. In the middle are two exquisitely worked wooden enclosures, one for the family and the other for the king. Evidence suggests that the monarch's chamber was commissioned for the visit of Charles I in 1625, a time when a plague in London led to Parliament being held in Oxford. Outside, a piece of tradition, rather than history, stands at the side of the chapel in the form of an ancient yew tree which has had a seat built round it. Here you could sit and ponder whether or not it really was planted to commemorate the coronation of King Stephen as long ago as 1135.

I chose the bench because of its simple shape and its sensitive positioning. It is the perfect place from which to look at this building. I was reminded that looking does require time and thought whereas 'seeing' does not.

MINSTER LOVELL HALL

On the banks of the River Windrush are the remains of a fifteenth-century manor house that takes its name from its first owner, William, seventh Baron Lovell of Tichmarsh.

As the vestiges of this sizeable baronial dwelling are spread over quite an area the initial impression is not one of a crumbling relic but of tall, elegant and seemingly unsupported walls that project into different planes. High window holes make shafts of light play over different shapes so that with the aid of fast-moving patchy clouds there is a strong feeling of movement that is in odd contradiction to a couple of centuries of dereliction.

Legend is the only repository of Lovell's fate. After fighting against the king as a supporter of Lambert Simnel he disappeared and is said to have made his way undetected to Minster Lovell. He was locked safely in a secret cellar to be fed daily by a loyal servant who took charge of the only key. However, the estate came to be seized by the king and the servant suffered either sudden death or banishment leaving his master to die incarcerated.

The final chapter in this macabre tale comes from workmen dismantling the house under the instruction of the Earl of Leicester. Quite by chance they came upon a secret chamber and just had time to glimpse the body of a man before it crumbled to dust with the sudden exposure to fresh air.

THE WHISPERING KNIGHTS

At around the time the pyramids at Giza were being constructed, the ancient Britons were positioning these stones to form a special chamber within a long earthen burial mound. Four thousand years after their efforts, this is what remains. This particular cluster forms one of three separate sites that are known together as the Rollright Stones. They are all within a few minutes walk of one another although I suspect the Knights attract least interest because they are a little way apart from the other two.

The fact that the fence protecting these stones is in pristine condition makes it seem all the more like a crown rather than some purely functional piece of iron-work. It also gives them the look of a modern piece of sculpture. The rough and solid forms of these stones are lovely to look at as the light plays across their weathered surfaces and I am sure this is what makes them particularly special to me.

DYING GLADIATOR AT ROUSHAM

Rousham is undoubtedly a special place. It is not one of those houses with canteens and strategically-placed gift shops which invariably turn a modest outing into a costly venture. Nor does it attract coach loads of tourists who might disgorge from their air-conditioned coaches and clutter up all in sight.

This may well be because Rousham is still a family home, that of the Cottrell-Dormers. Sir Robert Dormer, had it built in 1635 and his descendent, General James Dormer, was responsible for the foresight, a hundred years later, of employing an outstanding landscape architect by the name of William Kent. His speciality was in small, compact, landscape design incorporating backdrops of trees and hedges and plentiful use of follies and statues.

The gardens today are the only surviving example of his work that remain unspoilt and run right down to the banks of the River Cherwell. Aside from the interesting and considered layout of the grounds, the walk round the gardens brings into view all manner of statues and follies. Much of their impact is due to careful positioning so that in looking at them you are brought to rest at just the right spot to best see garden and artefact. This moribund performer is at the start of the walk round the garden and provides a strong preview of the style that lies ahead.

SAPLING

On the day this photograph was taken I went out specifically to get some pictures of Wychwood Forest. Only about five per cent of the land in Oxfordshire is woodland compared to well over sixty per cent arable so I thought it important to include this aspect of land use. As sometimes happens though it just did not work out. Either the sun was in the wrong place, the scene through the viewfinder looked boring or I could not find the right spot.

While I was heading off to look for a different area I spotted this sapling out of the corner of my eye. It was exactly what I was after: a simple shape. I thought about the slender lines of the tube that was providing protection and a safer micro-climate for this young tree. Also about that amount of care being given to a single plant, especially in relation to the tens of thousands that were to be sown behind. They were the agricultural equivalent of ephemera and would be well on the way to realizing their cash value by the time this cylinder was removed.

Motorways mean cars. Cars mean noise and pollution. And, if you believe the countryside to be a scarce resource, then these tarmacadam conduits also mean destruction.

The trouble is that they can also confer great advantages. On a basic level they often make travel easier, cheaper and quicker. This must be of some consequence in an age when, for whatever reasons, trade, business and individuals rely on mobility. There is also the point that what is lost by one environment is sometimes gained by another. Oxford, with its own formidable local traffic congestion, no longer has to be burdened with the passage of vehicles struggling to get up to the Midlands and beyond.

In terms of the appearance of the landscape, there can be nothing in the last seventy years that has made such an impact for the simple reason that we do not make many other things that are several hundred miles long. Thus, they are immediately worthy of record and enter into one of the most used functions of photography.

This picture was taken on a cold and pretty unpleasant day that seemed to me entirely the right conditions for recording what lay in front of me.

GODSTOW NUNNERY

Follow the River Thames, or Isis as it is known in Oxford, up past the station, through Port Meadow and you come to Godstow: a name that means 'God's place'. In doing this you will be making the same trip as Lewis Carroll when he told for the very first time the story of *Alice's Adventures in Wonderland*.

Set just off the river are the remains of a Benedictine nunnery, the reason behind this sojourn. From its foundation in the twelfth century to its destruction five hundred years later it was a place always linked to society's élite. No less a person than the king was present at the consecration of the abbey. Rosalind Clifford, the mistress of Henry II, became a nun here and in the Middle Ages it served as a finishing school for upper class young ladies.

Now, all that remain are the perimeter walls and the shell of the abbey. Nevertheless they have a commanding, yet gentle, presence which is somehow tempting to ascribe to their venerable past. The high walls, once a formidable barrier, now serve only to trap the last of the day's light and act like a beacon inviting you to wander within.

Disused Railway Near Cholsey

Even a cursory study of Ordinance Survey Maps for this area will reveal a large number of railway lines that are no longer in use. Driving through the country will frequently involve passing under emasculated railway bridges whose shining engineering bricks are all but covered by thick strands of ivy and thorny brambles. In most cases the track has been removed and vegetation has encroached to the extent that it is difficult to see where the line would have gone. This is one of the few places where the track remains and, as a result, the sense of loss is more apparent. Eroding concrete fence posts with exposed reinforcing rods testified to years of abandonment. Rails are no longer shiny enough to catch the light and wooden sleepers crumble under the weight of a boot.

Such decay may well cease. Recently, successful efforts have been made to get parts of the line running again so that once more plumes of steam and smoke can be seen moving through the landscape.

While walking along the track I found all sorts of interesting shots: clamps joining rails to sleepers, weeds growing over rails and longer shots of the line itself. However, the bridge attracted me most as it served to take my eye along the track. Framing the picture at an angle seemed somehow to be in sympathy with the movement of the carriages that had once polished the rails.

St Mary's Spire at Bloxham

Due north of Oxford and a few miles south-west of Banbury is Bloxham, its position marked for many miles around by the distinctive and stylish spire of this fourteenth-century church. This far north in the county the land has started to rise and the contour lines increase. Long-ranging views crop up all around the area making this church all the more of a landmark.

These features must have been of some consequence to the warring factions of the Civil War who saw a number of conflicts around the area. For instance, in 1645, only a year before the surrender of Oxford, it is reported that a sizeable force of Royalists set up in Bloxham as a result of poor strategy by the Parliamentarians in nearby Broughton Castle. Hearing that Royalist forces were already in Bloxham, a Colonel Fiennes withdrew his dragoons from Adderbury Bridge and so inadvertently gave them a safe route.

BURFORD

This venerable and picturesque wool town is often referred to as the gateway to the Cotswolds. It sits in the Windrush valley, due west of Oxford, not far from the border with Gloucestershire. The broad, steep High Street is a strong and unusual feature which runs down to the old river bridge at the bottom of the valley. Using present-day vernacular it could easily be renamed 'Antique Alley' as among the shops, pubs and houses that line each side are clusters of Volvos and Range Rovers. These generally indicate the presence of purveyors of polished and ancient artefacts: there are many here.

Just off the bottom of the hill is Burford Priory. Sir Lawrence Tanfield, Lord Chief Baron of the Exchequer to James I owned it after its original purpose, that of an Augustinian hospice. In the nineteenth century it was reduced to its present size and now functions as an Anglican nunnery. It is amusing, in view of its present use, to think that Charles II and Nell Gwynne are supposed to have stayed there. Today there is an Earl of Burford whose lineage traces back to that notorious relationship.

KELMSCOTT

On the western edge of the county and in the floodplain of the upper Thames is this distinctive, stone built village. A series of long straight roads cut through the flat lands of this part not unlike the centre of northern France. Such a route lends an appropriate feeling of remoteness which is confirmed by the single track road that leads only to the village.

A talented and extraordinary character lived here for over twenty years and undoubtedly caused the name of Kelmscott to be known far afield. He was the writer, craftsman, artist and social philosopher William Morris. His firm of decorators and interior designers, for which he is probably best known, produced original works of the highest quality in glass, fabric sculpture and woodwork. His partners, Ford Madox Brown, G.E. Street, Burne Jones and Rossetti have also moved into literature as examplars.

The sixteenth-century manor house, which was his home from 1871, sits at the back of the village, just off the circular road in the middle. It is open but only on certain Wednesdays. I particularly liked the solid, crafted feel of this village and the layout round the central piece of land that features in the photograph. The worked stone and solid houses seemed entirely appropriate to this rural and former home of such a craftsman.

WIDFORD

There is a haunting air surrounding this quaint and ancient church of St Oswalds. The church lies alone in these fields near the River Windrush a mile or so from the hamlet. It was built on the site of a Roman villa and so preserved the original mosaic floor, pieces of which can be seen near the altar.

With churches usually an integral part of the village layout, it was strange to come across this little hall of a church that could only be reached across the fields. Before I took this photograph I spent some time watching a surprising number of people walking across to visit. Even though for a period I was waiting for them to be out of sight I did like the idea of people making an effort to visit this relatively remote place of worship.

SPIRES OF OXFORD

Here is something of the skyline of contemporary Oxford, the like of which must have impinged on the mind of Matthew Arnold for him to have produced the all too often quoted line about the *dreaming spires* of Oxford.

As the name of this poet crops up so much in guidebooks on the city it is all the more apposite that his college, Balliol, should form the foreground of this photograph. It is also significant in being the college of the present Chancellor of Oxford University, Lord Jenkins of Hillhead. Furthermore, founded in 1263. it is arguably the oldest of the colleges. This particular claim is a contentious one so it should be pointed out that it is made on the basis of a functioning body of scholars having remained on the same site for the longest period.

The college had an interesting conception in that it began as the result of a penance handed out to the then Lord of Barnard Castle, John de Balliol. He was instructed by the Bishop of Durham to provide lodgings for impoverished scholars. At a spot not far from the present master's lodgings Balliol duly rented a house for this purpose. Unfortunately he did not live very long after his act of benefaction but his wife, Lady Devorguila, continued to support the venture providing the foundation for today's college.

Balliol and his devoted wife are buried together in the ruins of Sweetheart Abbey, near Dumfries, thereby forging an everlasting link with Scotland. This might well account for the particular affection I hold for this area of the city.

Pillbox Near Days Lock

This curious remnant of the last war is one of the few tangible reminders of the serious threat of invasion in the forties. They vary to some extent in size and shape depending on the strategic function and weaponry involved but all roughly conform to the shape that lent them their name.

As well as shape and novelty I was struck by the change in usage. How odd that an enclosure specifically designed to shelter soldiers and deadly armaments should now provide the same comfort for sheep and cattle. There was also a semantic aspect of interest. Cameras and guns share quite a number of words: barrel, trigger, pistol-grip, shoot, magazine, load, aim and even fire. The gun mount which presumably rested on the dirt inside would also have been but a sturdier version of my tripod.

It appealed to me, therefore, to consider the form of this hastily built emplacement, carefully frame what hitherto had been a deadly aperture and shoot with impunity.

RIVER THAMES AT SUTTON COURTNEY

It is hard to know whether Sutton Courtney should be called a small town or, more properly, a large village. The rural housing immediately gives it the feel of a village but the place extends to a size well beyond that of most such settlements. Either way it is an interesting place.

One of the many features is the church which, like many, is an amalgam of styles. Fourteenth- and fifteenth-century work predominate. Within the grounds are buried two well-known and contemporary figures. One is the writer George Orwell, less well known as Eric Blair. The other, Asquith, the former Liberal Prime Minister who also had a lesser known title, that of Earl of Oxford.

Somewhat overwhelmed by the number of pleasant cottages, I thought it would be nice to have a look at this backwater of the Thames which flows past to the north. It contributes a lot to the atmosphere of the place although rather more inconspicuous than other features.

EARLY'S MILL AT WITNEY

There is one word that is inextricably associated with the name of this town. It is 'blankets'. The link has developed with a reputation for fine blanket-making that began in the Middle Ages and runs on even now. The natural asset of the River Windrush, which flows through the town, is in many ways responsible. The quality of the water lends a unique softness to the blankets while its fast flow was ideal for powering water wheels that could drive the looms. Up until as late as 1837 the mills on the Windrush were powered by water rather than the increasingly prevalent steam-engine.

Although the town is no longer dependent on blanket-making it still has three mills, two of which bear the family name of Early. This firm of Charles Early (Witney) Ltd is the longest trading company in the United Kingdom and has in its records details of a presentation, in 1688, of gold-fringed blankets to King James II. The presentation was made by one Thomas Early.

The modern mill which now deals with production lies behind this chimney and out of sight, modestly tucked in behind the now redundant façade. This tall brick chimney, built almost a century ago, provides the only obvious clue to what has been a long history of weaving.

SWINBROOK

Here in the Windrush valley is what might be considered as one of the county's exhibition villages. It has a little babbling brook running through the centre, from which it gets its name, and even sports a brand new, old-style red telephone box: surely a contemporary measure of the worth of a place. This is Cotswold country without a doubt.

Aside from the obvious attractions of the surrounding geography, it is the thirteenth-century church of St Mary that is the focus of most attention. There is hardly a guidebook published that does not carry a photograph of the distinctive Fettiplace memorial depicting six reclining members of the family. At one time they were among the largest landowners of Oxfordshire and Berkshire. However, their line came to an abrupt end when, in the eighteenth century, four brothers died without producing children. St Mary's is also the final resting place of other well-known siblings, the author Nancy Mitford who died in 1972 and Unity Mitford who committed suicide so distraught was she at the death of her lover, Adolf Hitler.

Walking round the church itself I noticed the altar cross picking up the light and throwing it back out through the leaded window at the rear of the church. This is the image I took away with me that day and one that will remain in my mind.

SHOTOVER WOODS

These are the remnants of the once extensive Shotover Royal Forest that stretched over fifteen square miles. Forests of such special status were set up in Saxon times to provide exclusive hunting facilities for the king of the day. Indeed, there are records of the king's table at Windsor being supplied with venison from this forest. Boar were also hunted. Although perhaps apocryphal, there is an interesting story concerning a scholar of Queen's College who was attacked by such a wild animal. He was reading Aristotle at the time and, with remarkable presence of mind, saved himself by ramming the book down the animal's throat. This bizarre encounter is depicted in a stained glass window in nearby Horspath church.

Over the last three hundred years the forest has greatly diminished following its exemption from Forest Laws in 1660. The Civil War also exacted a cost when large numbers of oaks from the forest were used for both fuel and fortification. Without protection land was able to be bought and agriculture replaced woodland. Nevertheless, the woods that remain there today hold some beautiful walks through largely untouched forest.

As the only access is via a very steep hill virtually everyone nowadays arrives by car. When I thought about photographing the area I wanted to make some reference to this. Cars parked up conveyed nothing of the original scale of the forest so I was eventually attracted by this carefully arranged line of boulders that bordered a deeply pitted track and which kept vehicles at bay. This very track was at one time the main road into Oxford from the capital.

MAHARAJA'S WELL

There are many strange and fascinating sites in this part of England but this particular construction must qualify as one of the most bizarre. The well was opened in 1864 and utilized a four-foot-wide shaft, dug entirely by hand, that ran 368 feet deep. That is greater than the height of St Paul's Cathedral.

Edward Anderdon Reade, son of the Squire of Ipsden and Lieutenant-Governor General of the North Western Provinces of India is one of the central characters behind this construction. The other is the Maharaja of Benares who had close dealings with Reade before and during the Mutiny. It was as a gesture of thanks to him that the Maharaja donated this well in an imaginative act of philanthropy.

Not too dissimilar from a small Victorian bandstand the superstructure blends perfectly with its manicured rural surroundings. What appealed immediately was that unlike today's approach to engineering where design seems to focus on featureless and streamlined cowlings that hide functional components, the winding mechanism provides a key feature.

I was intrigued to read later on that its design had incorporated features that would lend themselves to photography. This struck me as being very far-sighted as part of a designer's brief of well over a hundred years ago.

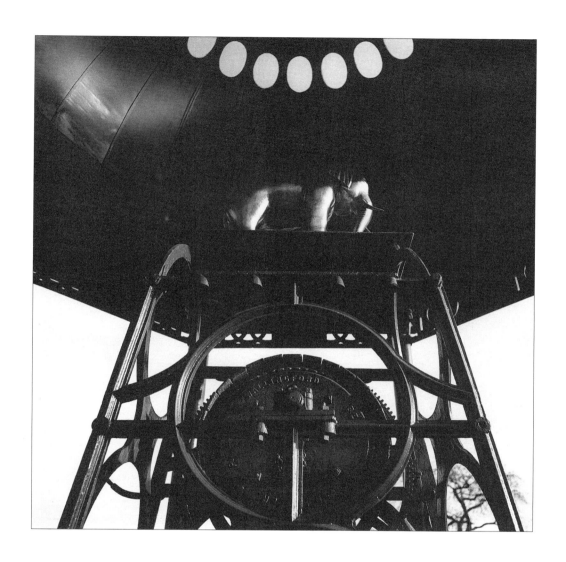

SHELDONIAN THEATRE

To the east of Broad Street, encircled by the bewhiskered, austere emperors, is the Sheldonian Theatre. The building was completed in 1669 having been designed by the then Savilian Professor of Astronomy, Christopher Wren. It is interesting to reflect that this was his first great architectural work.

In a number of ways this building occupies a unique position within the university as it is where all undergraduates enter the university during matriculation and finally receive their parchments. Here too, royalty, heads of state and eminent academics from across the world have passed under the ever watchful gaze of Melpomene to receive honorary degrees.

From a photographic point of view it presents quite a challenge in that, like all the main university buildings, it has been photographed a great many times. I wanted especially to convey the quiet solemnity that surrounds this venue of formal academia while at the same time making reference to some of the light that most of the undergraduates will have seen at the end of the tunnel.

POPLARS

Now and again it pays to look up. These trees invite just such a response. Long supple trunks allow them to bend gently in the wind and their small leaves give a gentle rustling accompaniment: a feature which is reflected in the name of the most common species of this genus, *Populus tremula*.

They are not particularly common in Oxfordshire, but where they do crop up is often along the edge of a narrow lane transforming it into a leafy corridor that is more reminiscent of Britanny than Britain.

Having looked upwards, the different dynamics become evident in that the top of the tree is moving far more than the bottom. This provides a good opportunity to incorporate movement in the photograph as a slow shutter speed will be sufficient to blur the leaves at the top of the frame while leaving the rest quite still. Movement shown in this way can often contribute to form: or perhaps it is the other way round.

KENCOT

The flat, upper Thames valley, between Lechlade and Witney, is the site of some remarkably picturesque villages that, with their neat stone-roofed cottages, wonderful gardens and freedom from major roads, set them apart in nature as well as location.

One of these is the village whose name appears under this carving of a dragon being slain by a centaur. It is a lovely piece of modern craftsmanship which reflects a twelfth-century carving in the nearby church of St George. Amid all the cosy antiquity of the area I was struck by the date at the bottom of the post which marked it as just under ten years old. I was, therefore, attracted by the idea of portraying the village through this contemporary piece.

Didcot Power Station

From an area that encompasses the furthest extent of the Chilterns to the west, the Cotswolds to the north and the full extent of the Berkshire Downs to the south these megalithic cooling towers can be seen. They send billowing, cumulous-like clouds of steam into the sky ensuring a formidable landmark whose presence is made known beyond the normal limits involving lines of sight.

Didcot is a major rail link, a feature noted back in 1914 by a high ranking War Office official who happened to be on holiday in the area. His observation made him aware of its suitability for the site of a large ordnance depot and led directly to it becoming the biggest military supply depot in Europe. The Royal Army Ordnance Corps remained at Didcot until 1963 when the run-down of the Services removed the need for the depot. Two years later, the Central Electricity Generating Board was looking for a site for a coal-fired power station and again saw the potential of this well-served position.

Originally I had wanted to get very close to the towers to make more of their shape but in the end I decided that the whole station, and its relation to the immediate surroundings, would be my choice. It was something of an accident that on the one day when conditions were right, there was no steam to be seen. Without the obvious evidence of their function I thought they began to take on more the appearance of curious monuments which, one day, might be the case.

BROUGHTON CASTLE

Without foreknowledge, this splendid moated Tudor mansion could easily be missed. It is partially obscured behind trees on the south-western edge of Broughton, a little iron-stone village a few miles south-west of Banbury. The situation is almost as fine as the building with a large open park sloping down towards the castle.

The original manor house was built by Sir John de Broughton at the beginning of the fourteenth century and was later owned by William of Wykeham, Bishop of Winchester and founder of New College, Oxford. It was his niece who provided the link with the next owner and direct descendent of the present owner, Lord Saye.

Just short of a century before the start of the Civil War, Richard Fiennes had the original mansion transformed into its present state. It would be in this building that his descendent met with leading roundheads to plot against Charles I.

Spitfire at RAF Benson

Like many of the surrounding counties, Oxfordshire was the site of a significant number of airfields during the Second World War. There were nearly two dozen operational stations and there will be many still who know of Oxfordshire through this context. Since 1939 when the base opened, it has developed a strong reputation. It was from here, for example, that the legendary de Havilland Mosquito, brought to popular attention through the film *633 Squadron*, made its operational début.

However, it is as the home of photographic reconnaissance that it first established its name. As well as the Mosquito, an equally-renowned aircraft, the Spitfire, was used to get pictures from such places as Bremen, Essen, Liège and Berlin. Of the great many crucial missions perhaps the most renowned was that of the 17 May 1943, for it was this that brought photographs confirming the success of the 617 'Dambuster Squadron' in breaching the Mohn and Sorpe dams. The aircraft pictured opposite is a replica of the original which stood to commemorate all from RAF Benson who served or lost their lives between 1939 and 1945. The original is now preserved in a display at the RAF museum in Hendon.

From the minute I saw this I was very keen to photograph it. The aircraft embodied a sense of style and design that came across so much stronger as a result of being mounted in an airborne position. When I was taking the pictures I had its former role in mind and thought it interesting that it was now the subject, and no longer the operator, of a camera. Thus it seemed appropriate to make use of the light and to minimize the impact of its terrestrial surroundings.

RIVER CHERWELL

This is the other river of Oxford and is known more for its beauty and leisure use than any commercial aspect. Apart from anything else it is too shallow and muddy. Its depth and tree-lined route make it an ideal site for punting between April and October and there is a particularly lovely stretch from the well-established Cherwell Boat House, in north Oxford, that runs through university parks and down towards the city centre.

This picture was taken some time before the punts were out and after a series of particularly heavy storms that caused the much swollen river to spill over its banks into the usually well-ordered and trimmed lines of this park. The scene made me very much aware of the way normally rigid boundaries can so easily change through the action of the seasons and therefore demand a fresh look. I was also pleased that I had caught something of the diversity of the river which adds so much to the character of the city.

ISLIP

There is an immediate sense of character to this place which must have something to do with the little hills on which it is built. There are narrow little streets that wind about giving unexpected glimpses of open landscape followed by the neat and tidy lines of village roofs.

This quiet feeling of atmosphere fits in well with the rich history that surrounds the village. Most people, for instance, will have some recollection of having read of Edward the Confessor if only because his title enables an easy mnemonic. He was born here almost a thousand years ago in the palace of his father, a monarch whose name, unlike that of his son, has not sustained popularity: King Ethelred. It was Edward who founded Westminster Abbey and forged a link in perpetuity with Islip by taking the novel step of bequesting the village to the abbey.

Much later, and as a result of the village's strategic position at the convergence of the Rivers Ray and Cherwell, Islip was the scene of much fighting during the Civil War. One of these conflicts involved Cromwell himself who, with nearly two thousand horsemen, overcame the Earl of Northampton and his forces: a defeat that took place in spite of Northampton having heavily reinforced as a result of intelligence on Cromwell's intentions.

This door is on the side of the church in the village centre. I invariably find doors of interest but here I found the simple lines and the equally unpretentious proportions made it lovely to look at. At the time there was much better light on another disused entrance but I felt that the lines here led to a stronger photograph.

THE MANGER

On the way up to White Horse Hill from Woolstone Hill you will probably want to stop for a minute or two to catch your breath. It is a good idea because in front of you, to the north-west, is the huge flat Oxfordshire plain and a view that, in area at least, is unsurpassed within the county's boundaries.

To the right of this expansive vista and below the Horse is a coombe called the Manger. It drops off the side of what must be the best kite-flying spot in the area. Although Thomas Hughes did not see it quite in this light, he was clearly impressed as this description from *Tom Brown's Schooldays* shows:

> Right down below the White Horse, is a curious deep and broad gully called the Manger, into one side of which the hills fall with a series of the most lovely sweeping curves; they are not a bit like stairs, but I never saw anything like them anywhere else . . .

The far-away edge of the Manger is called Dragon Hill and is reputed to be the sight where St George put to death the most famous fire-breathing reptile in western folklore.

The contours of this depression which so inspired Hughes provide a wonderful surface on which the light can play, particularly on a day such as this when hefty chunks of cumuli throw down shifting pools of light.

JOHN HAMPDEN MEMORIAL AT CHALGROVE

On this obelisk are marked the words:

> . . . Within a few paces of this spot he
> received the wound of which he died while
> fighting in defence of the Free Monarchy
> and ancient liberties of England.
> June 18 1643

Thus John Hampden, the great Parliamentary leader, was commemorated after his death in the battle of Chalgrove Field during the English Civil War. The Earl of Essex was defeated, Prince Rupert victorious yet again and Charles I's position maintained for a little longer.

Hardly an outstanding example of crafted stonework, the obelisk's featureless design is made all the more puzzling by a set of fortifications that are quite unique in my experience. To start with it is surrounded by a fearsome metal fence with jagged tops. This theme of protective ironwork is then continued around the pedestal by a threatening collar of angled spear-like poles which finally ensure its invulnerability.

For me the spiked metalwork was the most important feature and thus had to have a strong presence in the photograph. This unambiguous reference to pikestaffs and the flesh-piercing weaponry of seventeenth-century battle very nearly made up for the rest of the structure. Such were my thoughts until I made this print where-upon it dawned on me that the outer fence was very probably just a later addition, put there to protect onlookers from the perilous inner spikes.

CHARNEY BASSET GREEN

Legend, history and architecture are all features within the fabric of this village. The name 'Charney', for example, comes from 'Churn', the old name for the river that flows past the southern edge. It is now known as the Ock which in turn derives from a Celtic word for salmon, a fish that was plentiful here until the Thames became polluted.

A mile or so to the north of the village is the neolithic hill-fort of Cherbury Camp. As a Danish stronghold in the ninth century, legend holds that King Alfred spied on his adversaries while masquerading as a travelling minstrel. The intelligence he gained is meant to have enabled him to defeat them at Ashdown and Wilton. This is not the only apocryphal tale surrounding this site as another great king, Canute, is meant to have built a palace here.

There is less doubt though about Charney Manor. Built in the late thirteenth century it is one of the oldest surviving examples of the medieval manor house design. Its open H-plan is unusually exposed as there is no defensive moat and keep: a feature that is attributed to the protection that would have resulted from its close links with Abingdon Abbey

As for the green, its central position was often mirrored in the extent to which it featured in village life. Markets were held there, traditions enacted and news spread. Today it has to be guarded against being used as a car park.

THE MINISTER'S CAT

I would be very surprised if this cat did actually belong to a man of the cloth but I came across this little scene quite by chance and at a time when I had been reflecting on the nature of village life in Oxfordshire. At first my peripheral vision registered what I thought to be one of those life-like porcelain figures but a slight movement of the eyes revealed that I was being watched. Here was a piece of real life, still life that certainly typified an aspect of these surroundings.

Another reason I liked it is that it presented a good example of what can sometimes happen when you go out looking for pictures. Although you might have clear ideas about what you are looking for you should always be open to influence. Also, if you are ready, you will be able to photograph scenes that no amount of planning could make accessible. So it was that as I was packing up my camera and collapsing my tripod I noticed this feline form.

DITCHLEY LODGE GATE, BLENHEIM PALACE

It is no bland overstatement to say that Blenheim Palace and its 2,000-acre grounds, landscaped by Capability Brown, are magnificent. They are the home of the tenth Duke and Duchess of Marlborough and were a gift from Queen Anne to John Churchill, the 1st Duke of Marlborough, for his victory over the French at Blenheim. It took twenty years to build this royal benefaction during which time there was much debate and many changes.

One of these alterations concerned the main entrance and approach leading to the front of the palace. For any large building the main drive is obviously of some significance. In this particular case the palace itself covered no less than seven acres and the main drive, flanked by nearly seven hundred elms, was almost two miles long. How odd then that the Grand Avenue would be little used. It was pointing in the wrong direction, away from London. Today access to the grounds is from the Oxford road to the west of the palace.

Here at Ditchley Lodge Gate, to the north-west of the palace, is the spot that the designers envisaged as the threshold to one of the finest such creations in Europe, if not beyond.

BANBURY CROSS

It is funny to think that generations of children have bumped up and down on mothers' knees or drifted off to sleep to the sound of the famous nursery rhyme that talks of this monument and a horse. They would have had little cause to know that the original medieval High Cross was the target of puritanical zeal and destroyed around 1600: a measure of the extent to which Banbury and its environs embraced Puritanism. The cross pictured here commemorates the marriage of Victoria, Princess Royal, to Crown Prince Frederick of Prussia in 1858. At the time a number of locals were not happy that a religious symbol should be used and objections managed to delay it being built until 1859. The figures themselves, stoic and rather coldly opposed, were added in 1914 to commemorate the coronation of George V.

The town itself is a major centre for the northern end of the county and is second in size only to Oxford. The extensive industrial and commercial developments, particularly around the outskirts of the city, come as a bit of a shock after the agricultural land and small towns in the area. However, it has always been an important focus for trade and transport. In the late Middle Ages, for instance, the wool trade generated a lot of wealth and its strategic importance developed further with the Oxford canal reaching Banbury in 1778.

SATELLITE DISHES

What struck me most about these strange but increasingly commonplace shapes was the absolute incongruity. In a quiet rural area with rolling fields, twittering skylarks and bovine rumblings all around, this is not what might be expected. Giant satellite dishes picking up conversations that have been bounced off reflectors hundreds of miles above the Earth.

However, after the initial shock of witnessing this space-age scene, I remembered that the new technology of micro-wave communication has spawned the construction of a considerable number of receivers and transmitters that have acquired the status of landmarks. Anyone travelling regularly on the M40 to London for example is bound to use the tower at Stokenchurch as a measure of how the journey is progressing. Even at night television masts located on hills to the north-west of Oxford are conspicuous because of their flashing array of safety lights. So, these high-tech structures are now permanent features of our landscape and in most cases, because of the nature of their operation, away from settlements and occupying vantage points.

At least these dishes have been discreetly placed in a dip in the land but even if they were not I would find them interesting to look at. Perhaps it is because they are perceived as purely functional that they do not attract more appreciation.

STREET SIGN IN CROPREDY

I have always had a fascination for strange signs and like, if possible, to incorporate them in pictures. Recently this has extended to include odd street signs of which I now know there are an inordinate number. I was therefore delighted when I came across this splendid example quite by chance.

There was no obvious reason why such a strange name should appear and I could find no one able to give me an explanation. All I can say about it as a picture, therefore, is that it makes me laugh and reminds me of the potential for humour within photography. It can easily get taken far too seriously. There are not even any hidden or obscure references to beef up the 'meaning' as is often looked for. It is just a simple shot which I thought more than worthwhile to take, just because I liked it.

FARRINGDON FOLLY

As one of the last follys to be built in Britain, this structure is a relic of an endearing habit of those fortunate enough to have had spare land and wealth. It no longer seems to happen that such people choose to divert resources to preserving a whim in the form of a structure devoid of purpose. Perhaps the combination of tighter regulations on land-use with more alternatives for spending has put an end to such extravagancies. Whatever the cause, it is a loss.

Completed in 1935 the tower stands 110 feet and occupies an ideal position at the top of a mound just outside the town. Lord Berners commissioned it and involved Gerald Wellesley, 7th Duke of Wellington, in its design. There was quite a bit of opposition at the time earning it the tabloid epithet of 'Lord Berners' monstrous erection'. Running somewhat against what might be thought of as the definitive characteristic of follys, it proved useful as a look-out post during the last war.

Recent storms have meant that the folly is not nearly so obscured by trees so the shape is evident from a considerable distance. Up close, the brickwork becomes noticeable and all the more impressive a feat as course upon course demand a neck-bending view. Although a fine shot would be possible looking from the bottom of the hill, especially with the uncluttered slopes of the mound, I wanted to make full use of the folly's height to add strength of composition. I took quite a few shots with trees outlined on the sides but in the end felt that this simpler shot was the strongest.

ROMAN ROAD ON OTMOOR

About eight miles or so north-east of Oxford there is a four-thousand-acre stretch of open fenland that is in sharp distinction to any other piece of land in the county and quite probably unique in this part of the country. It has been recorded that the Romans built a road through it around AD 40 and with typical ingenuity made foundations of brushwood to cope with the marshy conditions caused by the River Ray and its tributaries. This photograph was taken within the moor and on that very road and as such is something of a record of the age of this remote area.

Controversy over the use of land has meant that Otmoor has frequently been the scene of violent protests. The law of enclosure was responsible for most of these scenes as, for example, when the Duke of Marlborough petitioned Parliament in 1810 for the enclosure of the moor. In this case, just the act of putting up notices to this effect brought violence against the men involved. Five years later though, an act to drain and enclose the moor became law. Then in 1829 serious unrest developed. It began with the arrest of infuriated farmers who, after flooding had covered prime farmland, destroyed dykes to let the river follow its old course. Although acquitted, the case unleashed the resentment over the despised enclosure. For the following three years something close to guerilla war broke out between locals and landowners to the extent that a request was made for the government to send troops. The request was denied but it was not until a detachment of police arrived from London that order was restored.

More recently a road, other than the one photographed, led to further controversy. It was the route of the M40, the invasive rumblings of which have now defied the experts' predictions and spoil the stillness.

EWELME

Brick and flint have been used to build this village giving it a distinctive tone and feel that is quite different to the yellow and brown colours of iron and limestone that are so common throughout the county. It sits just below the Chiltern escarpment and is surrounded by rolling countryside. An Old English word for 'spring' or 'source of a river' gives the village its name. This stream also provides the village with exceptionally fine watercress, beds of which are harvested and, up until recently, taken down to Covent Garden where the cry of 'Ewelme Cress' was a well-established sound.

Up a steep bank, is a unique complex of medieval church, school and almshouses which have remained virtually unchanged since they were built in the middle of the fifteenth century. They were built by the Duke of Suffolk and his wife Alice Chaucer, granddaughter of the renowned poet, Geoffrey. Inside the church is another relic of this family in the form of the poet's son, Thomas Chaucer, who was constable of Wallingford Castle and speaker of the House of Commons in 1414.

Steps at the base of the church tower take you down to the quiet cloister of the almshouses which are even today supported by the funds Alice Chaucer left in 1475. The buildings have been sensitively preserved and so easily convey an atmosphere redolent of their ancient beginnings.

DEAD TREE NEAR NORTH LEIGH

At the top of a field that runs down to the banks of the River Evenlode is this dead tree. There is nothing particularly significant about its position, it plays no part in local folklore nor does it look as if it might be unusually old. But in spite of this and its perished form it did make me stop immediately and take this photograph.

The backdrop of flat, hedge-lined fields is typical of much of this county and must contribute to the cosy feel of the place. This is not a land of bleakness or rough drama but instead is one of extensive agriculture, gently changing relief and a generally tidy order that fits well with the remnants of history that crop up almost everywhere. Indeed, not a mile away are the remains of a Roman villa that still display a mosaic floor, laid at the beginning of the fourth century.

ARDINGTON HOUSE

On reading the name of this building it brought to mind what might be thought of as an anglicized version of the fictional and now almost legendary home of Drs Cameron and Finlay. The only similarity, however, is an acoustic one. The style is early Georgian so that it has a pleasing sense of formality and proportion without being foreboding. Distinctive in its own unassuming way, it stands as a pleasant reminder of the many big houses that are to be seen on wandering off off the beaten path by just a few miles.

Part of the historic buildings association and open during the summer, it was once the home of Lord Wantage who held land in the area of over 47,000 acres. Aside from his title and position as major landowner, he is remembered for his action in the Crimean War where he won the Victoria Cross.

Ardington itself is just off the old Roman road known as the Portway which runs east from nearby Wantage. This was probably considered superior to the older Ridgeway which was much more exposed.

UFFINGTON

At the edge of the flat plains, just before they rise up into the hogs-back escarpment known as the Ridgeway, is this chalk and brick-built village that houses what is known locally as the Cathedral of the Vale. This is the thirteenth-century church of St Mary, the curious octagonal tower of which is a striking landmark of the area. This adjective is well suited for in 1740 the spire which it then had was destroyed by lightning.

The church also features in the life of the village's most famous inhabitant, the author of *Tom Brown's Schooldays*, Thomas Hughes. He spent much of his youth here in the care of his grandfather the Revd Dr Hughes who was vicar of Uffington for seventeen years from 1816. Prior to this, the last stage in his distinguished life with the church, Dr Hughes had been tutor to the family of George III and Canon of St Paul's Cathedral.

HAMPTON GAY

This little hamlet dates back to Saxon times and relied on agriculture until the second half of the sixteenth century. It was then that the now ruined Manor House was built and the emphasis began to shift from the land. The manufacture of paper became the main source of revenue when the old water mill was converted to this purpose around 1700. Further modernization a hundred and fifty years later added a gasworks and steam engine that boosted production to a ton a day.

On Christmas Eve in 1874 Hampton Gay became the scene of a disaster. A London train bound for Birmingham took on passengers and an extra coach at Oxford. This last carriage became derailed at Kidlington but the train carried on dragging it as far as Hampton Gay where it finally crashed through the bridge and into the freezing water of the River Cherwell. Villagers rushed down to help and were quickly joined by others, including Lord Randolph Churchill who had driven over from Blenheim Palace. Thirty-four people died and over a hundred were injured.

Thirteen years later disaster returned. This time the village was not merely the site of tragedy but also the victim. The paper mill was closed, removing the livelihoods of virtually all the villagers. In the same year the Manor House was gutted by fire, never to be rebuilt.

There is now no trace of the mill and Hampton Gay has shrunk back to the size it was in medieval times. With such a chequered history and with so little trace, I was drawn to the ruins of the Manor House. They are on private land so there was a limit to how close I could get. Nevertheless in the circumstances it seemed fitting to view this derelict mansion from a respectful distance.

LITTLE WITTENHAM NATURE RESERVE

Although only 250 acres this little reserve contains a wealth of interesting features not least of which is an excellent vantage point that gives views of the Chilterns to the east, the Cotswolds to the north and the Ridgeway to the south. It is called Round Hill, from where this picture was taken, and is the base for the well-known cluster of beeches, Wittenham Clumps.

About six hundred yards south-east there is Castle Hill, the site of an iron age hill-fort. The ditch at the base of the hill formed part of the defences and would have been dug over two thousand years ago. Although the hill has never been systematically excavated, discoveries from when the area was farmland suggest the hill was the focus of a reasonable-sized settlement.

On the day I climbed to the top of the Clumps I watched a thunderstorm advance from the north. Before the deluge that followed I came upon this wee sign with its kind warning. Its last word, wavering in the wind, drew my attention to the vast cooling towers in the distance, Didcot power station, and made me laugh.

The Northmoor Trust

Little Wittenham Nature Reserve

Manor House, Little Wittenham, Abingdon, Oxfordshire OX14 4RA.   Tel: (086) 7205 7780

WARNING
THIS FENCE IS
ELECTRIFIED

DISUSED AIRFIELD AT STANTON HARCOURT

It has always fascinated me the way nature reclaims unattended buildings. Vegetation starts appearing in the most unlikely places, starting perhaps with sproutings in safe and well-nourished guttering. Mosses then begin to blur the lines of neat window panes and even the sloping surfaces of roofs end up supporting a range of flora like the once well-attended beds below. The order and definition no longer reflect man's careful control but instead mark the abandonment that often follows a change in priorities.

Such natural regression is all the more poignant when evident on the site of an area hitherto characterized by order and control. Fifty years ago even flaking paint on a door would have warranted a rebuke to someone.

Now what remains is a relic of Second World War operations: one of the nearly two dozen airfields that were operational in the county at that time. This building, serving now as a shelter for goats and farm machinery, was once used to dry out parachutes.

Such notions would have been far from the minds of those men who saw the attack in 1940 by three German bombers which suddenly appeared over Stanton Harcourt. Nine people were killed and as a result these defences were built. Perhaps it is a good metaphor that, like memories of all the killing, these buildings should gradually fade away.

GREAT MILTON

Tradition maintains that the poet John Milton came from this town and even that 'Paradise Lost' was penned here, although for this last claim at least there seems to be little supportive evidence. Whatever the truth, Milton's family were certainly familiar with the area. His father was ranger of the nearby Shotover Forest and there are connections with two other villages in the area, Stanton St John and Forest Hill.

Nowadays the village is known by many more as the site of 'Le Manoir', an exclusive hotel and French restaurant run by the well-known chef, Raymond Blanc. This is close to the church where the village seems to jump up in scale, predominated by large houses with spacious grounds. In contrast are the small houses in the centre of the village around the green and the row of cottages that line the way in. These little houses seemed far more friendly and neighbourly than their grandiose counterparts further up the village and this struck me as a good feature to have along an entranceway.

STONESFIELD

Here is a town whose name, rather more than most, relates to its history. It lies in the Evenlode valley which runs west of another town with a building material incorporated in its name: Woodstock.

The majority of stone roofing slates used in the north of Oxfordshire, and for many of the colleges, were mined from this town. A large number of mines were in operation, the last closing just before the First World War. Although nearly eighty years has passed, there are still open shafts within the town. They go down so deep that on a cold morning the hot air from below produces a steady flow of steam.

It was temperatures at the other end of the scale that were of consequence to the miners. After the stone, or pendle as it was known, had been hauled up from the shafts it was covered with soil to await a frost. As temperatures dropped, the stones would be uncovered to allow the frost to split the stones into slates which could then be trimmed to shape for roofing.

The only really accessible evidence of these workings is in a wood just south of the town. Here can be seen piles of trimmings and stones that had been mined but never used. This picture was taken on a day when temperatures were around freezing and the woodland was alive to the sound of melting ice and dropping snow, not unlike the sounds that must have prevailed as stone sheered into slates.

BINSEY

Binsey is a small village to the north-west of Oxford. It is not the normal type of village in that there are no shops, post office or even public telephone: amenities that, in part at least, are supported by even the most meagre hamlet. Most people come across Binsey on their way to a well-known pub, the Perch, which backs on to the Thames as it flows through Port Meadow. However, others may well pass through it as they go to visit the church of St Margaret which is further up the lane. In the grounds is to be found the Binsey Treacle Well, a place of pilgrimage in the Middle Ages and more recently referred to by Lewis Carroll when, at the Mad Hatter's tea-party, the dormouse recounted the tale of three children who lived at the bottom of a treacle well. The only English pope, Adrian IV, is said to have been incumbent at Binsey in his earlier years.

ORCHARD AT KINGSTON BAGPUIZE

This is an example of somewhere that will not be mentioned in any of the guide-books but is, nevertheless, well worth a look. This orchard has been going since 1936 and produces four varieties of pears and eighteen varieties of apples.

The frost-covered strands in between the trees are asparagus. Asparagus originated from the birds who had come to feed on the apples and has now spread throughout the orchard. This variety is older and therefore more flavoursome than that commonly available. It does, however, compete with the limited water supply so there is a fine balance to be maintained. Apples too have a reputation for a particularly fine flavour. As nearly 70 per cent are sold from the orchard there is no pressure to pick prematurely, to allow for storage and prevent overripening, as can happen with much larger orchards that supply supermarkets.

With the proliferation of massive supermarkets that is so much in evidence, smaller concerns must be struggling to survive. Taking just the example of English orchards over 5 acres, the numbers have dropped in the last four years by over 150 to 859. It might, therefore, be prudent to recognize these smaller and more human outlets as being under threat and, in words prominent in all small post offices, 'use it or lose it'.

CHURCHILL

Such a name will forever be associated with this county; however, this village is but a namesake of the eminent family based some twelve miles to the south-east at Blenheim Palace. It lies towards the north of the county, a few miles off the western perimeter road that runs up from Swindon to Banbury.

Unlike many of Oxfordshire's smaller villages this one has seen a great deal of alteration, largely about a hundred years ago under the patronage of Squire John Haughton Langston. Such was his beneficence that he had this church of All Saints built at his own expense. Relatively modern, it was consecrated in 1827. The design of the tower is of special interest as it is an exact replica of the tower of Magdalen College, Oxford, differing only in being two-thirds the size of the original. After having seen Magdalen Bridge and the adjoining college tower, this extraordinary architectural *déjà vu* asks strongly to be the hallmark of this fascinating village.

WAYLAND'S SMITHY

The construction of this burial chamber very probably pre-dates the oldest parts of Stonehenge by a thousand years. Considering that our year is just short of the second millennium Anno Domini this site can properly be called ancient: an adjective that, in this case in particular, merits some attempt at quantifying.

Originally with a stone floor and wooden roof it served as a gallery grave for fourteen people. It was later modified to have two side chambers and was found to contain eight bodies from which the heads had been separated.

The name 'Wayland' was given by the Anglo-Saxons and refers to the Viking myth of the great smith of that name. Wayland was said to be the owner of a white horse and legend has it that any traveller whose steed had lost a shoe need only leave his horse and a coin at the entrance for it to be shod by Wayland's magic.

While trying to decide how I would photograph this I was struck by the reactions of the sightseers that came along to view this piece of history. The majority did not seem to want to spend any time at all looking at it, far less explore its considerable size. Instead they appeared happiest either to be photographed standing beside the entrance or quickly scanning a video camera over the scene. I thought it sad that the very instrument I was using to try and enhance perception seemed to be having the opposite effect. I took this photograph while pondering over the moral in that observation.

The White Horse

Were it not for the revision of county boundaries in 1974 this, arguably the most famous of hill-figures in Europe, could not be included in this book.

Often with sites of such antiquity it is difficult to offer precise dates and this is no exception. While these lines by G.K. Chesterton foster legend rather than fact they are perhaps worth reading:

> Before the gods that made the gods
> Had seen their sunrise pass
> The White Horse of the White Horse Hill
> Stood hoary on the grass

The Department of the Environment tries to be a little more precise and puts its construction at around the first century. Others say that Alfred had it constructed after his victory over the Danes in the ninth century. But a preoccupation with dates is not my concern nor why I am glad of the change in boundaries. Above all else, this stylized and beautifully proportioned horse is a magnificent spectacle that needs no historical rhetoric to establish its importance.

Its complete form can really only be seen from about a mile away, thus all the more remarkable a feat of artistry. The skill involved in construction impressed me most so I wanted to highlight the abstraction involved at the bare surface.

ALMSHOUSES AT LYFORD

This tiny rural village sits on the southern bank of the River Ock and is reached down an appropriately diminutive road signposted 'Lyford Only'. These 'only' signs, as I think of them, invariably lead to worthwhile discoveries if only because the destination is so quiet. This is no exception.

Lyford Grange, over on the east side of the village, entered the history books as the site of a fatal betrayal. This happened in 1581 when a much-hunted Jesuit preacher, by the name of Edmund Campion, was captured there. His arrest led to torture and imprisonment in the Tower of London before being subject to the ternary and lethal mutilations that frequently followed.

I chose to photograph these sixteenth-century almshouses because I found their fine sense of order and neatness immediately appealing. I also liked the scale that came with the buildings but felt it odd that the clock should be so large in relation to its surroundings. When framing this particular shot I was tempted to react against the order and symmetry that so characterized the place but after a short while my first reactions predominated. This suggested a simple and central shot that did not rest on an imbalance.

THE SECRET FOREST, WYCHWOOD

This is one of England's expansive medieval forests which in the past used to be one of the largest royal hunting areas covering over a hundred thousand acres and stretching out as far as Burford and Witney. Today only about two per cent of that survives which is quite a thought to have while wandering through what is still a sizeable forest. Large though it may be, much is private but there are clearly marked areas for walking.

The law of enclosure took its toll on the forest and from this record it would appear that not only the trees were affected:

> Nor is it in the view of productiveness alone that such an imnclosure is to be wished: the morals of the whoile surrounding country demand it imperiously. The vicinity is filled with poachers, deer stealers, thieves and pilferers of every kind . . . and Oxford gaol would be uninhabited were it not for this fertile source of crime.

The middle of the nineteenth century saw the removal of the legal status of forest with much of the land being turned over to agriculture. In 1862, 1,500 acres were enclosed and passed to the owner of Cornbury Park and it is this that remains.

Before taking this picture I had taken a number of others outside the forest but was not very pleased with the results and felt I was too preoccupied with showing what the forest looked like. The frustration quickly disappeared when I followed the footpath inside the forest and got close to the trees. I felt that a detail was, in the end, more illustrative than a view from afar.

HENLEY ON THAMES

This is another of Oxfordshire's towns that has an international reputation. Apart from the beauty of the place it must be the annual regatta that spreads its name. Set up in 1839 it starts during the first week in July and runs along one of the widest and longest stretches of the river between the main bridge and Temple Island to the north.

There are many things to see here but I felt the river had to feature somehow, especially as it also formed the county boundary. Not a great deal is immediately accessible apart from a stretch that runs south from the main bridge towards the lock. Walking along here you get an interesting cross-section of life in Henley that ranges from the lush and exclusive riverside houses to the rather more active municipal park. Cruising sedately along the river are extravagant vessels that look as if they would be more suited to sailing out the Florida Keys in search of equally out-sized fish. But there are also diminutive little outboard-powered craft that doubtless give the owners just as much pleasure despite there being no room for a well-stocked drinks cabinet.

This launch, which also embraces the river in its name, was for me the strongest image I came across. Its mooring, with the classic backdrop, says a lot of what Henley is about. The boat also managed to get across style and a touch of extravagance without recourse to a large scale, and that appealed.

Oxford Canal at Thrupp

The Oxford canal flows alongside this little village which once was home to barge-workers who brought coal and industrial products down from the Midlands. The canal was finished in 1790 and remained an important routeway for the next hundred years. However, increasing competition from the progressively faster and cheaper railway system led to its decline so that in 1955 the Banbury to Oxford section was officially closed to commercial traffic.

Although the industrial side has disappeared the canal is far from a sterile stretch of water. It now provides a home for a significant number of people many of whom have taken great care in converting the old barges into homes. Their individual and colourful liveries are reassuring reminders that traditions can be preserved.

GUIDE POST NEAR WROXTON

Little is known about this except that it was commissioned in 1686 by a Mr F. White. In those days it was not the responsibility of the local council to provide such posts. Those that did get positioned were the result of collections made by local villagers or, as seems likely in this case, gifts from benefactors. Perhaps one of the oldest such posts in the country, this has twice had the attentions of craftsmen restorers in recent years: 1975 and 1983.

It was interesting to compare this lovely piece of sculpture with the bare utility of its contemporary counterpart on the other side of the road. At first I thought of framing them together for such a comparison but this could only be done at the expense of details on the stone. Everybody knows what modern signs look like so I thought the shot would be stronger from a closer viewpoint. I also judged the background to be distracting so decided to look up to the sundials which, in the afternoon light, gave the right time.

DORCHESTER ABBEY

In several books it is written that of all the historic places in Oxfordshire, Dorchester is the most significant. It was, for instance, the Saxon capital of Wessex. In the seventh century Pope Honorious charged a Benedictine monk by the name of Birinus to convert the West Saxons. The monk was clearly successful in his task because he ended up baptizing King Cynegils and his entire court in the River Thame, a tributary of the Thames.

The Augustinians were responsible for building the abbey and started construction some eight hundred years ago. In common with a lot of medieval churches its present form evolved over a great many years. The Norman nave is the oldest feature while the sanctuary was added in the fifteenth century. One thing not to miss is the unique Jesse window in the north end of the abbey which has been in place for five centuries. In these days of high power fund raisers, with their many inducements, it is interesting to note that on the opposite side to this magnificent window are the family shields of those who contributed to its cost.

On this same point of fund raising, it is worth having a look at the outer face of the tower for a corbel with a surprisingly modern visage. It is that of Edith Stedman, an American, who first came to Dorchester in 1954. From her extraordinary efforts money has been raised to create the Abbey Gardens, restore the east window and convert the former Guest House into a museum. With so much going on I thought it best to go for an obtuse view of this fascinating building.

BEECH WOOD AT CHRISTMAS COMMON

Sitting on top of the Chilterns, close to the Ridgeway and surrounded by beautiful beech woods, this is an area that attracts what I think of as 'serious walkers'. I have always thought of this sub-species as being most considerate so, within such a small village, I was surprised to see such a number of well-crafted notices about parking. Although still polite, their brief and succinct messages left no room for ambiguity and gave the impression of having been drafted only after much abuse had taken place.

Four roads converge here, despite its name there is no common and the corridor-like arrangement of houses mean that visitors are quite conspicuous. It is probably best, therefore, that the village is admired and left in peace. This I did but was pleased to be able to walk in the woods as I wondered whether or not there really had been so many stiff notices.

GREAT AND LITTLE HASELEY

Like Tweedle Dum and Tweedle Dee, Great and Little Haseley are almost one in both likeness and location. Only a mile or so separates them and both induce numerous kind epithets and would certainly give a committed urbanite something to think about. This link also has a tangible form in the wood that separates the two villages. Its name, Haseley Wood, is hardly surprising but it is a nice reminder of the meaning of the place names, namely 'hazel wood'.

It is Great Haseley though that most is written about, probably because of its fine church and long line of distinguished rectors one of whom was father to the famous architect, Christopher Wren. Despite this focus of attention I was more interested by the minor village.

A narrow little road runs through the village on its way to its namesake. There are no obvious traffic signs, no pavements, no yellow lines and expanses of grass on both sides lead up to definitive country dwellings where maintenance has given way to manicure.

Before coming here I had never photographed a daffodil, let alone a whole group of them. But in this setting I thought it worth having a go as they contributed so much.

MARTYRS' MEMORIAL

In these days of church leaders working for a stronger ecumenical movement it is difficult to imagine the vehemence of feeling that once existed between Roman Catholic and Protestant factions. Only in Northern Ireland do we get a frequent and sad reminder of the lives that are lost due to allegiance to one or other side.

However, in the centre of Oxford stands this ornate memorial, erected to mark the deaths of an archbishop and two bishops who were burnt at the stake only a couple of hundred yards from where the monument stands. Although the executions took place well over four hundred years ago the base of the memorial is still a favourite site for proselytizers who, through all weathers, project their message against the noise of the traffic.

The most senior of the martyrs, Thomas Cranmer, had already been convicted three years before of treason on two counts and had been sentenced to be hung, drawn and quartered. His fate was delayed though in order that Queen Mary could have him condemned for the more serious crime of heresy. His last stand was with his two colleagues, Nicholas Ridley, Bishop of London, and Hugh Latimer, Bishop of Worcester. At a specially organized religious court they failed to argue their theological stance, refused to recant their position and were thus condemned as heretics. Such was the mood against these Protestant clergymen that a special bill was brought before Parliament to re-enact the statue prescribing death by fire for heretics. Cranmer was made to watch the burning of Ridley and Latimer before suffering the same fate five months later.

BOAT-HOUSE AT SHILLINGFORD

Here is an example of how traditional building styles embrace the riverine side of Oxfordshire life. Although the emphasis is now very much on leisure travel up and down the Thames, with much of that traffic on hired craft, there are a large number of houses along its route where the boat-house is arguably of more consequence than the garage. This is particularly the case south of Oxford where the river widens and more exclusive properties border the Thames.

Shillingford is just a little place about ten miles south of Oxford, rather more on the river, which has an unusually stylish bridge that carries the A429 over the river.

I liked the quiet of this particular spot, set on a bend, with a bench thoughtfully positioned at the end of the road from which to look at the opposite bank and watch the river traffic go by. I was struck by the way the reflected afternoon sun picked out the slats on the doors to give them an abstracted version of the wash on the river below.

PORT MEADOW

On the north-west side of Oxford lies this flat expanse of land that has enjoyed special status for almost a thousand years. The Domesday Book mentions it as a place where all the Freemen of Oxford have a common pasture outside the city wall. They had the right to graze horses and cattle, but not sheep, and this still persists today. Another conspicuous animal presence comes in the form of geese. Originally, geese were kept at nearby Wolvercote and brought to the river each day to drink. Inevitably their interest strayed from the river towards their wild counterparts leading to a hybrid by the name of Port Meadow Special.

Never having been ploughed, the ground provides a unique habitat for flora such as floating sweet-grass, water mint and Oxford ragwort. The land has since been designated a Sight of Special Scientific Interest which might well help to preserve its undisturbed state.

Whatever else, it is used and much valued as an area for recreation. Kite-flying, walking, riding, fishing and flying model aeroplanes all take place without it ever seeming crowded: except that is, when it freezes. Word seems to get round with astonishing speed so that by lunch-time the scene is reminiscent of a Breugel painting. Hundreds of people are to be seen skating, making slides or just taking in the spectacle.

PHOTOGRAPHIC NOTES

All the photographs were taken on a 500 CM Hasselblad using either a 50 mm, 80 mm or 150 mm lens. Most of them involved the use of a tripod and cable release but where the camera was hand-held it is marked with an asterisk on the following table.

In almost all cases the film used was Ilford FP4 with modifications made to standard development times based on lighting conditions. The only filters used were red or orange to compensate for the inability of panchromatic film to distinguish between blue and white. Clouds are therefore able to feature more strongly.

While the following table might be of interest it should not give the impression that knowledge of a certain combination of lense, film, shutter speed and aperture provide the key to taking improved pictures. It is the one disadvantage of such information and therefore surprising to see these details given so much prominence in many publications about photography.

Leaving aside the key aspect of perception, the most important considerations are composition, correct exposure and the ability to print. In terms of the finished photograph, there is no chance of capturing what is seen unless the film has been correctly exposed. And in turn, even with a correctly exposed and developed negative from which to work, making the print is a separate area of expertise.

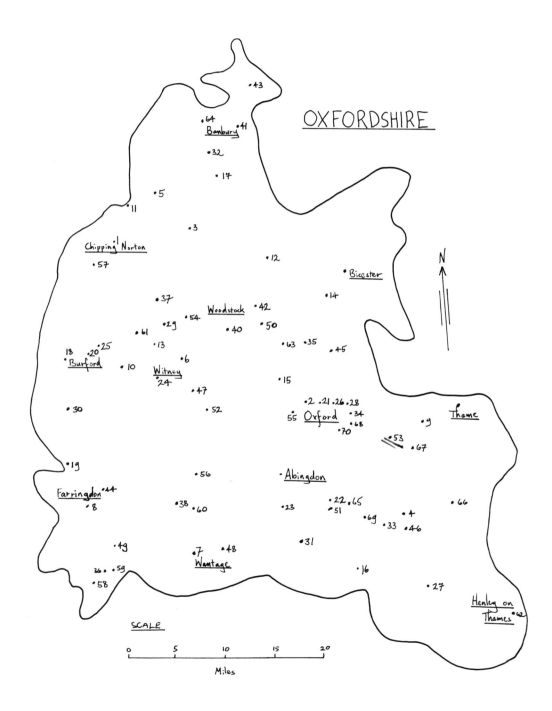

OXFORDSHIRE

N

• 43

• 64
Banbury • 41
• 32
• 17
• 5
• 11
• 3
Chipping Norton • 1
• 57
• 12
• Bicester
• 37
• 14
Woodstock • 42
• 29 • 54 • 50
• 61 • 40
• 63 • 35
18 • 20 • 25 • 13 • 45
Burford • 6
• 10 Witney • 15
24
• 47
• 2 • 21 • 26 • 28
• 30 • 52 55 Oxford • 34 Thame
• 68 • 9
• 70
• 53
• 67
• 19
• 56 Abingdon
Farringdon • 44
• 8 • 38 • 60 • 23 • 22 • 65 • 66
• 51 • 4
• 69 • 33 • 46
• 31
• 49
• 7 • 48
36 • • 59 Wantage
• 58 • 16
• 27
Henley on
Thames • 62

TECHNICAL DATA

All photographs were taken on a 500 CM Hasselblad. Those that were taken hand-held are marked with an asterisk.

PAGE NO.	MAP NO.	TITLE	LENS	SPEED	APERTURE	FILTER
2	1	BLISS'S MILL AT CHIPPING NORTON	150 mm	1/2	f32	orange
4	2	ASHMOLEAN MUSEUM	50 mm	1/15	f22	orange
6	3	GREAT TEW	80 mm	1/8	f22	orange
8	4	SIGN POST	80 mm	1/8	f16	orange
10	5	HOOK NORTON BREWERY	50 mm	1/2	f22	orange
12	6	NORTH LEIGH	150 mm	1 sec	f32	orange
14	7	ALFRED THE GREAT AT WANTAGE	50 mm	1/2	f22	red
16	8	THE GREAT BARN	50 mm	1/4	f22	none
18	9	RYCOTE CHAPEL	80 mm	1/15	f11	none
20	10	MINSTER LOVELL HALL	50 mm	1/4	f22	orange
22	11	THE WHISPERING KNIGHTS	50 mm	1/4	f22	orange
24	12	DYING GLADIATOR AT ROUSHAM	80 mm	1/15	f11	orange
26	13	SAPLING	50 mm	1/15	f8	orange
28	14	M40	50 mm	1/15	f22	orange
30	15	GODSTOW NUNNERY	50 mm	1/15	f22	none
32	16	DISUSED RAILWAY NEAR CHOLSEY	50 mm	1/2	f22	none
34	17	ST MARY'S SPIRE AT BLOXHAM	150 mm	1 sec	f32	orange
36	18	BURFORD	50 mm	1/15	f11	none
38	19	KELMSCOTT	50 mm	1/2	f22	orange
40	20	WIDFORD	150 mm	1/2	f32	none
42	21	SPIRES OF OXFORD	150 mm	1 sec	f32	orange
44	22	PILLBOX NEAR DAYS LOCK	80 mm	1/2	f22	orange
46	23	RIVER THAMES AT SUTTON COURTNEY	50 mm	1/2	f22	orange
48	24	EARLY'S MILL AT WITNEY	80 mm	1/4	f22	orange
50	25	SWINBROOK	50 mm	1/15	f11	none
52	26	SHOTOVER WOODS	50 mm	1/4	f22	orange
54	27	MAHARAJA'S WELL	50 mm	1/125	f5.6	none
56	28	SHELDONIAN THEATRE	50 mm	1/8	f22	orange
58	29	POPLARS	50 mm	1/4	f22	orange
60	30	KENCOT*	80 mm	1/125	f5.6	orange
62	31	DIDCOT POWER STATION	150 mm	1 sec	f32	red
64	32	BROUGHTON CASTLE	80 mm	1/2	f22	orange
66	33	RAF BENSON*	50 mm	1/125	f8	orange
68	34	RIVER CHERWELL	50 mm	1/15	f22	orange
70	35	ISLIP	50 mm	1/2	f22	none
72	36	THE MANGER	80 mm	1/2	f22	orange
74	37	JOHN HAMPDEN MEMORIAL	50 mm	1/2	f22	orange
76	38	CHARNEY BASSET GREEN	50 mm	1/8	f8	orange
78	39	MINSTER'S CAT	80 mm	1/60	f5.6	none
80	40	DITCHLEY LODGE GATE, BLENHEIM PALACE	50 mm	1/4	f22	none
82	41	BANBURY CROSS	50 mm	1/15	f22	red

PAGE NO.	MAP NO.	TITLE	LENS	SPEED	APERTURE	FILTER
84	42	SATELLITE DISHES	80 mm	1/4	f22	orange
86	43	STREET SIGN IN CROPREDY	80 mm	1/60	f5.6	none
88	44	FARRINGDON FOLLY	50 mm	1/2	f22	orange
90	45	ROMAN ROAD ON OTMOOR	50 mm	1/8	f22	orange
92	46	EWELME	80 mm	1/30	f8	none
94	47	DEAD TREE NEAR NORTH LEIGH	50 mm	1/15	f11	orange
96	48	ARDINGTON HOUSE	50 mm	1/4	f22	none
98	49	UFFINGTON	50 mm	1/30	f8	orange
100	50	RUINS AT HAMPTON GAY	80 mm	1/4	f22	orange
102	51	LITTLE WITTENHAM NATURE RESERVE	80 mm	1/125	f5.6	none
104	52	DISUSED AIRFIELD AT STANTON HARCOURT	80 mm	1 sec	f16	orange
106	53	GREAT MILTON	150 mm	1/2	f32	none
108	54	STONESFIELD	50 mm	1/2	f22	none
110	55	BINSEY	50 mm	1/15	f22	orange
112	56	ORCHARD AT KINGSTON BAGPUIZE	50 mm	1/15	f11	none
114	57	CHURCHILL	50 mm	1/8	f22	orange
116	58	WAYLAND'S SMITHY	80 mm	1/4	f22	orange
118	59	WHITE HORSE*	50 mm	1/125	f5.6	orange
120	60	ALMSHOUSES AT LYFORD	50 mm	1/4	f22	orange
122	61	THE SECRET FOREST, WYCHWOOD	80 mm	1/15	f11	none
124	62	HENLEY ON THAMES	80 mm	1/8	f16	none
126	63	OXFORD CANAL AT THRUPP	80 mm	1/15	f22	orange
128	64	DIRECTION POST AT WROXTON	80 mm	1/15	f16	none
130	65	DORCHESTER ABBEY	50 mm	1/30	f8	orange
132	66	BEECH WOOD AT CHRISTMAS COMMON	80 mm	1/2	f22	none
134	67	GT. AND LITTLE HASELEY	50 mm	1/2	f22	orange
136	68	MARTYRS' MEMORIAL	50 mm	1/4	f22	orange
138	69	BOAT HOUSE AT SHILLINGFORD*	50 mm	1/125	f8	orange
140	70	PORT MEADOW	50 mm	1/125	f8	none